WRITTEN AND COMPILED BY

*Jax Berman*

 PETER PAUPER PRESS, INC.
White Plains, New York

*To all the unicorns
in the world.*

Designed by Heather Zschock

Illustrations © LenLis,
used under license from Shutterstock.com

Copyright © 2018
Peter Pauper Press, Inc.
202 Mamaroneck Avenue
White Plains, NY 10601 USA
All rights reserved
ISBN 978-1-4413-2841-0
Printed in China
7 6 5 4 3

Visit us at www.peterpauper.com

# INTRODUCTION

Human beings are fascinating creatures.
We're born with boundless potential with the
entire world to explore and influence...
yet between meetings, commutes, routines,
and the rest of our perfectly mundane
day-to-day lives, it's easy to forget just
how powerful and magical we are.

Within the pages of this pocket-sized tome,
you'll find magic: witty and pithy fragments
of wisdom from a variety of wordsmiths,
designed to remind you that there is a spark
of magic within each and every one of us, just
waiting to be awakened. Whenever you need
a little reminder that you are just as powerful
and unique as the elegant unicorn, reach for
this book, flip it open, and let its words
reignite the sparkle within you.

Always be
yourself.
Unless you can
be a unicorn.
Then always be
a unicorn.

UNKNOWN

THE UNIVERSE IS
FULL OF MAGIC THINGS,
PATIENTLY WAITING
FOR OUR SENSES TO
GROW SHARPER.

EDEN PHILLPOTTS

The impossible just takes longer.

DAN BROWN

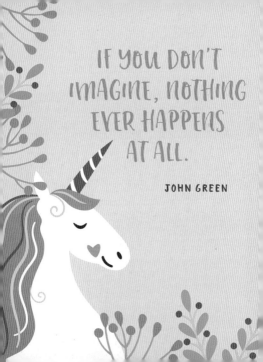

IF YOU DON'T IMAGINE, NOTHING EVER HAPPENS AT ALL.

JOHN GREEN

Sometimes things become possible if we want them bad enough.

T.S. ELIOT

So many things are possible just as long as you don't know they're impossible.

NORTON JUSTER

A DREAMER IS ONE
WHO CAN ONLY FIND HIS
WAY BY MOONLIGHT,
AND HIS PUNISHMENT
IS THAT HE SEES THE
DAWN BEFORE THE REST
OF THE WORLD.

**OSCAR WILDE**

The magic is you
can change more
things than you
could ever dream of.

**STEPHEN FURST**

WHY, SOMETIMES
I'VE BELIEVED AS
MANY AS SIX
IMPOSSIBLE
THINGS BEFORE
BREAKFAST.

**LEWIS CARROLL**

Whatever you can do,
or dream you can,
begin it.
Boldness has
genius, power,
and magic in it.

W. H. MURRAY

I believe I'm a unicorn.
Unicorns are very magical
and powerful and strong.

**JUSTINE SKYE**

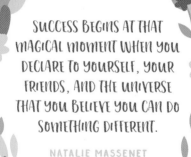

SUCCESS BEGINS AT THAT
MAGICAL MOMENT WHEN YOU
DECLARE TO YOURSELF, YOUR
FRIENDS, AND THE UNIVERSE
THAT YOU BELIEVE YOU CAN DO
SOMETHING DIFFERENT.

NATALIE MASSENET

Life is a
magical
thing.

LAUREL CLARK

*Desire* is creation, is the magical element in that process.

If there were an instrument by which to measure desire, one could foretell achievement.

WILLA CATHER

THE HUMAN RACE IS A
VERY, VERY MAGICAL RACE.
WE HAVE A MAGIC POWER
OF WITCHES AND WIZARDS.
WE'RE HERE ON THIS EARTH
TO UNRAVEL THE MYSTERY OF
THIS PLANET. THE PLANET IS
ASKING FOR IT.

YOKO ONO

Make no little plans; they have no magic to stir men's blood and probably themselves will not be realized.

**DANIEL BURNHAM**

# THE POWER OF IMAGINATION MAKES US INFINITE.

JOHN MUIR

USE THE POWER
OF YOUR WORD IN
THE DIRECTION OF
TRUTH AND LOVE.

DON MIGUEL RUIZ

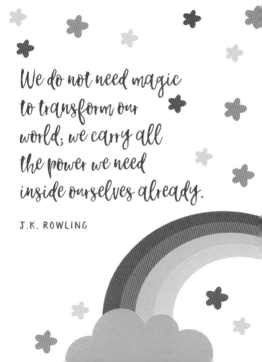

We do not need magic
to transform our
world; we carry all
the power we need
inside ourselves already.

J.K. ROWLING

EACH PERSON HOLDS SO
MUCH POWER WITHIN
THEMSELVES THAT NEEDS
TO BE LET OUT.
SOMETIMES THEY JUST NEED
A LITTLE NUDGE, A LITTLE
DIRECTION, A LITTLE SUPPORT,
A LITTLE COACHING,
AND THE GREATEST THINGS
CAN HAPPEN.

PETE CARROLL

You may not
realize this, but
people have the
power to change
the world.

MORRISSEY

HOPE CAN BE A POWERFUL
FORCE. MAYBE THERE'S NO
ACTUAL MAGIC IN IT,
BUT WHEN YOU KNOW WHAT
YOU HOPE FOR MOST AND HOLD
IT LIKE A LIGHT WITHIN YOU,
YOU CAN MAKE THINGS HAPPEN,
ALMOST LIKE MAGIC.

**LAINI TAYLOR**

Visions are worth fighting for. Why spend your life making someone else's dreams?

TIM BURTON

CHERISH YOUR VISIONS
AND YOUR DREAMS AS
THEY ARE THE CHILDREN
OF YOUR SOUL, THE
BLUEPRINTS OF YOUR
ULTIMATE ACHIEVEMENTS.

NAPOLEON HILL

Hope lies in dreams, in imagination, and in the courage of those who dare to make dreams into reality.

JONAS SALK

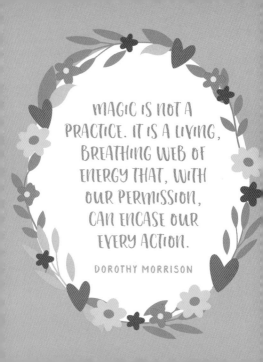

MAGIC IS NOT A
PRACTICE. IT IS A LIVING,
BREATHING WEB OF
ENERGY THAT, WITH
OUR PERMISSION,
CAN ENCASE OUR
EVERY ACTION.

DOROTHY MORRISON

Anyone who
doesn't believe
in miracles is
not a realist.

DAVID BEN-GURION

Hope makes people good, a lot of the time. You hope for a brighter future, and resentment is outweighed.

**DAISY RIDLEY**

MAGIC EXISTS. WHO CAN
DOUBT IT, WHEN THERE ARE
RAINBOWS AND WILDFLOWERS,
THE MUSIC OF THE WIND AND THE
SILENCE OF THE STARS?
ANYONE WHO HAS LOVED HAS
BEEN TOUCHED BY MAGIC.
IT IS SUCH A SIMPLE AND SUCH
AN EXTRAORDINARY PART
OF THE LIVES WE LIVE.

**NORA ROBERTS**

HOPE IS NOT A
RESTING PLACE BUT
A STARTING POINT—
A CACTUS, NOT A
CUSHION.

H. JACKSON BROWN, JR.

Hope is a
waking dream.

ARISTOTLE

If you have a dream, don't let anybody take it away, and always believe that the impossible is possible.

SELENA QUINTANILLA

NOTHING IS BLACK OR WHITE,
NOTHING'S US OR THEM.
BUT THEN THERE ARE
MAGICAL, BEAUTIFUL THINGS
IN THE WORLD. THERE'S
INCREDIBLE ACTS OF KINDNESS
AND BRAVERY, AND IN THE
MOST UNLIKELY PLACES,
AND IT GIVES YOU HOPE.

DAVE MATTHEWS

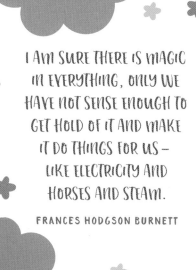

I AM SURE THERE IS MAGIC
IN EVERYTHING, ONLY WE
HAVE NOT SENSE ENOUGH TO
GET HOLD OF IT AND MAKE
IT DO THINGS FOR US —
LIKE ELECTRICITY AND
HORSES AND STEAM.

FRANCES HODGSON BURNETT

If you can dream it, you can do it.

ENZO FERRARI

ALL HUMAN BEINGS
ARE ALSO DREAM
BEINGS. DREAMING
TIES ALL
MANKIND
TOGETHER.

JACK KEROUAC

That's the beginning of magic. Let your imagination run and follow it.

PATRICIA A. MCKILLIP

Men at some time are masters of their fates: the fault...is not in our stars but in ourselves.

**WILLIAM SHAKESPEARE**

"THAT'S ONE FORM
OF MAGIC, OF COURSE."
"WHAT, JUST
KNOWING THINGS?"
"KNOWING THINGS
THAT OTHER PEOPLE
DON'T KNOW."

**TERRY PRATCHETT**

HAVE A DREAM,
CHASE IT DOWN,
JUMP OVER EVERY
SINGLE HURDLE, AND
RUN THROUGH FIRE
AND ICE TO GET THERE.

**WHITNEY WOLFE**

To accomplish great things, we must not only act, but also dream; not only plan, but also believe.

ANATOLE FRANCE

IS THERE MAGIC IN THIS WORLD?
*Certainly!*
BUT IT IS NOT THE KIND OF
MAGIC WRITTEN ABOUT IN FANTASY
STORIES. IT IS THE KIND OF MAGIC
THAT COMES FROM IDEAS AND THE
HARD WORK IT OFTEN TAKES TO
MAKE THEM REAL.

**ROBERT FANNEY**

NEVER UNDERESTIMATE
THE POWER OF DREAMS
AND THE INFLUENCE OF THE
HUMAN SPIRIT.

**WILMA RUDOLPH**

This world
is but a
canvas to our
imagination.

HENRY DAVID THOREAU

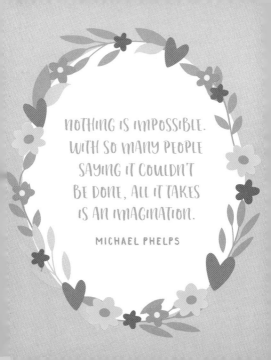

NOTHING IS IMPOSSIBLE.
WITH SO MANY PEOPLE
SAYING IT COULDN'T
BE DONE, ALL IT TAKES
IS AN IMAGINATION.

MICHAEL PHELPS

Imagination is the only key to the future. Without it none exists — with it all things are possible.

**IDA TARBELL**

YOU SEE THINGS;
AND YOU SAY
WHY?
BUT I DREAM THINGS
THAT NEVER WERE;
AND I SAY
WHY NOT?

GEORGE BERNARD SHAW

EACH OF US HAS AN INNER
DREAM THAT WE CAN
UNFOLD IF WE WILL JUST
HAVE THE COURAGE TO
ADMIT WHAT IT IS. AND THE
FAITH TO TRUST OUR OWN
ADMISSION. THE ADMITTING
IS OFTEN VERY DIFFICULT.

**JULIA CAMERON**

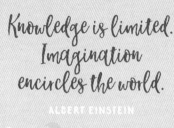

Knowledge is limited.
Imagination
encircles the world.

**ALBERT EINSTEIN**

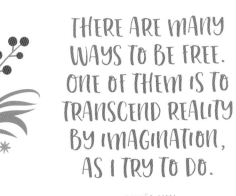

THERE ARE MANY
WAYS TO BE FREE.
ONE OF THEM IS TO
TRANSCEND REALITY
BY IMAGINATION,
AS I TRY TO DO.

ANAÏS NIN

Beware,
for I am fearless
and therefore
powerful.

MARY SHELLEY

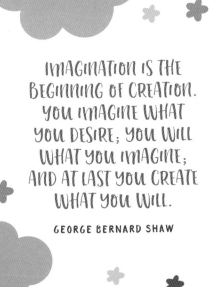

IMAGINATION IS THE
BEGINNING OF CREATION.
YOU IMAGINE WHAT
YOU DESIRE; YOU WILL
WHAT YOU IMAGINE;
AND AT LAST YOU CREATE
WHAT YOU WILL.

GEORGE BERNARD SHAW

Without leaps of imagination, or dreaming, we lose the excitement of possibilities. Dreaming, after all, is a form of planning.

GLORIA STEINEM

If one is lucky
a solitary fantasy
can totally transform
one million
realities.

MAYA ANGELOU

IT IS ENTIRELY CONCEIVABLE
THAT LIFE'S SPLENDOR FOREVER
LIES IN WAIT ABOUT EACH ONE
OF US IN ALL ITS FULLNESS,
BUT VEILED FROM VIEW,
DEEP DOWN, INVISIBLE, FAR OFF.
IT IS THERE, THOUGH,
NOT HOSTILE, NOT RELUCTANT,
NOT DEAF. IF YOU SUMMON IT BY
THE RIGHT WORD, BY ITS RIGHT
NAME, IT WILL COME.

**FRANZ KAFKA**

We are magic.
It is magic that
we're walking
around.

**DONOVAN**

THAT'S THE THING
WITH MAGIC.
YOU'VE GOT TO KNOW
IT'S STILL THERE,
ALL AROUND US,
OR IT JUST STAYS
INVISIBLE FOR YOU.

CHARLES DE LINT

THE IMAGINATIVE CHILD
WILL BECOME THE IMAGINATIVE
MAN OR WOMAN MOST
APT TO CREATE, TO INVENT,
AND THEREFORE TO
FOSTER CIVILIZATION.

L. FRANK BAUM

Stuff your eyes with
wonder, live as if you'd
drop dead in ten seconds.
See the world.

RAY BRADBURY

So many of our dreams
at first seem impossible.
And then they seem
improbable. And then when
we summon the will, they
soon become inevitable.

CHRISTOPHER REEVE

IF YOU HAVE BUILT CASTLES
IN THE AIR, YOUR WORK
NEED NOT BE LOST; THAT IS
WHERE THEY SHOULD BE.
NOW PUT THE FOUNDATIONS
UNDER THEM.

**HENRY DAVID THOREAU**

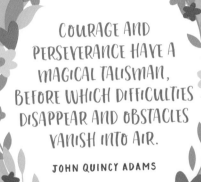

COURAGE AND
PERSEVERANCE HAVE A
MAGICAL TALISMAN,
BEFORE WHICH DIFFICULTIES
DISAPPEAR AND OBSTACLES
VANISH INTO AIR.

JOHN QUINCY ADAMS

Magic comes
from the heart,
from your feelings,
your deepest
expressions of
desire.

**JIM BUTCHER**

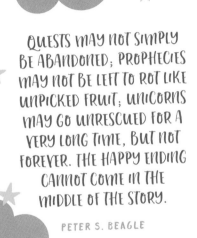

QUESTS MAY NOT SIMPLY BE ABANDONED; PROPHECIES MAY NOT BE LEFT TO ROT LIKE UNPICKED FRUIT; UNICORNS MAY GO UNRESCUED FOR A VERY LONG TIME, BUT NOT FOREVER. THE HAPPY ENDING CANNOT COME IN THE MIDDLE OF THE STORY.

PETER S. BEAGLE

Beauty, happiness,
they're things so big
they can't capture them
with their scientific
words. It's like what they
used to call magic.

**HEATHER ANASTASIU**

HE COULD LEAP THE CORRAL,
IF HE ROSE
TO HIS FULL WHITE HEIGHT;
HE COULD SPLINTER THE
FENCING LIGHT,
WITH THREE BLOWS
OF HIS PORCELAIN HOOFS IN
FLIGHT—IF HE CHOSE.
HE COULD SHATTER HIS
PRISON WALL,
COULD ESCAPE THEM ALL—
IF HE ROSE,
IF HE CHOSE.

**ANNE MORROW LINDBERGH**

Courage is the magic
that turns dreams
into reality.

**ASTER LAKER AND RICHTER ABEND,**
*TALES OF SYMPHONIA*

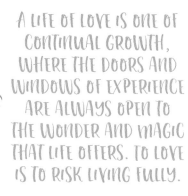

A LIFE OF LOVE IS ONE OF
CONTINUAL GROWTH,
WHERE THE DOORS AND
WINDOWS OF EXPERIENCE
ARE ALWAYS OPEN TO
THE WONDER AND MAGIC
THAT LIFE OFFERS. TO LOVE
IS TO RISK LIVING FULLY.

LEO BUSCAGLIA

Love works magic.
It is the final
purpose
Of the world story,
The Amen of the
universe.

NOVALIS

"WELL, NOW THAT
WE *HAVE* SEEN
EACH OTHER,"
SAID THE UNICORN,
"IF YOU'LL
BELIEVE IN ME,
I'LL BELIEVE IN YOU."

LEWIS CARROLL

It's a rare gift,
to know where you
need to be, before
you've been to all
the places you don't
need to be.

URSULA K. LE GUIN

Some things have to be believed to be seen.

RALPH HODGSON

And above all, watch
with glittering eyes the whole
world around you because
the greatest secrets are
always hidden in the most
unlikely places. Those
who don't believe in
magic will never find it.

ROALD DAHL

I DEFINITELY BELIEVE THAT
YOU ARE DRAWN TO CERTAIN
THINGS FOR INEXPLICABLE
REASONS, BUT IN A VERY
POWERFUL WAY. I DON'T KNOW
WHAT IT IS EXACTLY, BUT I KNOW
THAT THINGS HAPPEN KIND OF
MIRACULOUSLY SOMETIMES,
AND SO I'M WILLING TO BELIEVE
THAT THERE'S SOMETHING
PRETTY MAGICAL OUT THERE.

RACHEL MCADAMS